CRY FROM THE HEART

Poems

By

LEONARD KOLOKO

CRY FROM THE HEART

ISBN: **978-1-4716-9027-3**

Pulished by Lulu

Cover Design: L Koloko

CONTENTS

Acknowledgements

The following poems have been previously published on the 'Poems Corner' of the ***Sunday Mail,*** a national weekly newspaper: *'Look Out', 'Whose Child', 'Care for Us', 'The Road', 'Lonely Child', 'Change for the Better', 'Man on Earth', 'Rope of Hope', 'Song from the Needy', 'If I had known', 'Girls of the Night', 'Ashamed'* and *'Girl Child Blues'. 'Hungry Soil'*, which constitutes *two poems 'Grave Waste'* and *'Old Serpent of Sodom'*, appeared in ***National Mirror,*** a Christian newspaper; *'Whose Child'* has also appeared in the African poetry anthology **'Echoes Across the Valley',** published by East African Educational Publishers (2000), Nairobi, Kenya. *'Song from the Needy', 'Ode to a Mother'* and *'No longer at Ease'* have been published on Lulu.Com (formerly Poetry.com) and in an International Poetry Library anthology 'Letters from the Soul'. It also opened my play 'Kanayaka' recited by a six year old Tsepo Kabange. *'If I had known'* has had a public reading at an International youth festival held in Sweden by Zambian theatre actor Kennedy Phiri. A good number have also had readings on Radio Ichengelo, a Zambian catholic station by broadcaster Ian Mpundu Mwansa.

Special thanks to Mr. Wilson Tembo, who first read through and evaluated most of these poems and for his encouraging comment. He wrote:

"These are well written poems to soothe the injured and give courage to the timid."

PREFACE

My poetry is a set of personal thoughts brought forth in a creative manner; rhythmically, lyrically and inspirationally. It is borne of the heart and aims to reach out to other hearts.

My sole aim for offering the world this collection is to share the love I have in my, sometimes, introvert heart and mind. This love transcends all barriers of race, religion, tribe, social class, gender and nationality.

Poetry is one art many want to ignore but it stares in our faces right from the beginning of life. Mothers coo soothing lullabies' to the newly born; kindergarten teachers use nursery rhymes to teach the young ones; musicians use lyrics to convey their messages in song; lovers sing out romantic poems to each other and death is celebrated with eulogies.

Life's diverse issues are tackled in this collection. These pieces are for the lonely souls; the orphans, street children and HIV/AIDS victims. Read, enjoy and share.

Leonard Koloko
Kitwe, Zambia.
October 2011

1. IF I HAD KNOWN

If I had known
I wouldn't have dared
If I had known
I could have cared
But useless me
I dared and never cared.
If I had known
I wouldn't have tried
And for sure they wouldn't have died.
If I had known they were flirts
I wouldn't have accepted their dates
But careless me
I went about dating and flirting.
Today I sit and regret
Crying over spilt milk
And I whisper
"If only I had known."

2. LOOK OUT!

Look out!
Not for the looks
Not for the money
But for AIDS
It has come to kill.
Cherish the friendship
Cherish the partnership
But watch your step
For relationships may spell your doom.

Look out!
Many have fallen
Many have died
Because they did not care,
They flirted about and cared not to use condoms.
Look out for the flirts
They change partners like skirts.

Look out!
Watch your step
There's more to life
Than meets the eye.

❖

3. LOVE HURTS

Jenny said she loved me
She gave me her lips
We kissed at will.
She gave me her breasts
I fondled them well.
I played with her on the lawn,
And loved her till dawn.

Jenny said she loved me
I swallowed her words
Sweet and tasty they were.
Jenny said she loved me
And I said I loved her too
But foolish me,
I never knew she loved another.

4. SOLITUDE

A minute of silence please
Let it tick
For time never waits.
A time for memories please
Let it pass
For it is now a part of us
Indeed many have departed.

5. WHOSE CHILD

I, who roams the streets,
Eats from refuse bins
And sleeps in the gutter,
Whose child am I?
I, who sniffs petrol,
Puffs dagga,
And begs around in town,
Whose child am I?
I, who was thrown in the latrine,
Still born,
Deprived of a life
Beyond my embryonic state
Whose child would I have become?

6. THE ROAD

No one knows where it comes from
No one knows where it ends
We just roam on it and follow where it leads.
On our way we stumble and fall
At times we grow mighty and tall
Sometimes we are lonely and unloved
Other times we are occupied with friends and love.
Worry not about this road
We shall reach our destiny before dusk.

7. ODE TO A MOTHER

Mother,
You anchored the embryonic me
In the oceans of non-existence.
You felt me evolve
From mere celluloid,
To flesh and blood.
In pain you felt me
Slipping out into this world,
You watered me with the milky rain of your breasts
And beamed on me your
Sunshine love.
Mother,
You watched me grow
From my crawling
To my toddling;
From my walking
To my running.
And here I am running for life.

8. ASHAMED

Come by my side
Come let us hide
Like Adam and Eve
Let us hide our shame.
The park was our Eden
Where we felt so secure and hidden
Daily we met there
To play games bare.
You let me search your treasures
Just to fulfill my lusty pleasures
I took refuge in your territory
And was so sure of my victory.
I won the game
But it has led us to shame,
Am I to blame for this new fame?
I am too young to play father
And you are too young to play mother
Yet here we are joining parenthood
Long before our own adulthood

9. *CRY FROM THE HEART*

A cry from my heart
Sharp and hurting
Tears me apart.
A cry from my depth
Heavy and tiring
Tears me to death.
Life hurts,
Life is heavy;
Lord I carry this load
Heavy with thoughts,
Heavy with tribulations.
A cry from the heart
Silent and mild
Makes me feel like a child
Lost in a forest of trials and tribulations.

10. POETIC LOVE

It takes a little time
To write a poem in rhyme.
You need a lot of patience
To understand the essence.
Love is likewise
It is not so easy to visualize,
Though present in the prudent and the wise.

11. GIRL CHILD BLUES

I am just a child
Please leave me
I am just a child I need to be free.
My breasts are just sprouting
It's a path to my tender growth
they are not for you to tickle and fondle.
I am just a child
Please let me be.
I am just a child
I am crying to be free.
Yes, my hips have began to curve
It's a way of my tender growth
they are not for you to touch and feel.
I am just a child
and I mean just that.
I am just a child
and I have my own rights
I need to be freed from all
Abuses and plights.

12. HIS WAY

Stop!
There are hazards in your way,
Sharp stumps and deep pot holes,
Sharp thorns,
And rough stones.
Be steady!
And watch your steps.
Stop, my friends.
Stop and follow His Way to salvation.

13. PERHAPS TOMORROW

Pass by little bee
Float on
Secure and free.
Perch on little bird
Sing your song,
Don't let it fade.
Raise your head
Little flower
Let me be your lover.
Perhaps tomorrow
Little bee
I'll find you safe and free,
Perhaps tomorrow little bird,
I'll still find you singing
The same sweet song.

14. FATE

Fate has favored me less,
Leaving me lost and lonely.
I sprouted from the soil
Not knowing the seed which started me,
From the soils of my origins
I was uprooted
And transplanted to new soils.
I shed orphan's tears
And shudder with an illegitimate child's fears
For I know not who really I am.

15. NATWANGE! (Let's rejoice, tomorrow we die)

Natwange!
For the sun is bright,
Touching us with its warmth and light.

Natwange!
For wind is ghostly
Blowing in us so calm and softly.
In us throbs the drumbeat of life
In us we feel our hearts dancing alive.
In the heat of the sun
We sweat
So precious are the beads of our sweat,
We lick the salty drops
So sweet their taste.
So today we are a live
We love, we hate
We smile, we frown
We rejoice, we mourn
And tomorrow we die.

Natwange!
For the sun dies not,
The wind blows us to another destiny.

16. LONELY CHILD

Sometimes I have wondered
Whether I was born to be lonely
I have wondered
Whether anyone cares about me,
They all look too busy to notice me.
They've all gone to satisfy their own needs,
Mother to the kitchen party,
Father to the pub,
Brother to the disco,
Sister to the party.
Here I sit all alone
So neglected, so forsaken.

17. DAWN

The sun reappears
Over the eastern horizon,
Its golden rays touching mother earth,
Warmly with its love.
Flowers raise their open petals,
 Receiving the sun's warm kiss.
Birds awaken from their nests,
Singing along to natures beautiful love song.
We awaken too,
From yester-night's nightmares,
Dress up,
And brace for today's struggles.

18. BUTTERFLY

Look at that butterfly
Floating on the wind,
See the beauty of its wings
Beautiful thing
Let it be.
Let it float on the winds of your thoughts,
Let it pass, let it pass.
Let it search for nectar
For that's its life.

19. MAN ON EARTH

Man on earth
Is a caged bird
Locked up in torment by evil.
He pretends to be happy
When sadness rules his life,
He acts sane when he is insane.
Where love grew, he uprooted
And sowed hatred.
Where freedom was planted, he slashed
To grow slavery.
Where peace brewed, he now boils war.
Why was man created?
Was it to dwell in lunacy?

20. SLEEP

I shut my eyelids
To rest my eyes
From the evils of the day.
My mind functions anew in a world of darkness
and peace.

21. IF ONLY

The heart misses
The mind wishes
If only time can wait.

22. CHANGE FOR THE BETTER

You rain insults on me
When I cry to be free
You call me many a name
When I try to save you from shame
You want to live in danger
As if you are a total stranger
Change for the better, brother
Change for the better, sister
You say I am wasting my time
Fighting against your crime
You call me a fool
Taking things so cool
Change for the better, brother
Change for the better, sister

23. RUNNING MY RACE

Time elapses
Ticking a life synopsis
One second, two seconds…
In my prime I can't beat the time.
I am running a race
Sweating profusely in the face,
I can't keep pace with this time and space.
There's no one to cheer,
But everyone to jeer;
There's no one to embrace,
But everyone to disgrace
Yet still,
I keep on running.

24. MY REPENTANCE

Lord I return
Face cast down
Tied up in a frown
Streaming with repentance tears.
Down my heart boils guilt
I know it is my entire fault
My heart is hardened by sin.
On my knees I sink
Face lifted up
Lips whispering a prayer of repentance.
Down my heart
Suddenly shines your love
Softening it with your salvation.
Lord I return
Face bright with a smile
Eyes streaming with joyful tears
I feel so new.

25. AND SO …

And so
Black and white
Mixed
And dropped into the crystal clear ocean;
And so East and West
Fused
To defuse their Atomic bombs.
And so
Protestants and Catholics
Fellowshipped t together
And reunited in Christ.
And so Muslims and Christians
Knelt together
And prayed for world peace.
And so
Me and myself
Became one to restore my sanity
In a world so full of insanity.

26. WEEP NOT CHILD

With sorrow I cry
Burying my torment for tomorrow
I wish I was not born in this world of trouble torn.
'Help me lay a wreath on his lonely grave,' to the wind I whisper.
Not an echo I hear.
The place is so silent
Vanished ones are now dumb souls.
In the shadow of life
Lingers my searching soul
I can't find my lost ones
Silently I sob for them.
'Weep not child,
For there's birth,
there's death,'
so the wind sings to me.

27. DREAMS

They come
They go
They rise
They fall
They blossom
They falter
Just in one generation.

28. IS IT REALLY ME?

Is it me, really me?
Walking so proud,
Walking so free?
Is it me, really me?
Walking like king,
Worrying no more of a single thing?
Is it me, really me, whose cheeks were battered
 and face spat at?
Is it me, really me, who was verbally abused
wrongly and falsely accused?
Time really flies,
Injustice really dies.
Is it me, really me,
healed of a tormenting child abuse?

29. SONG FROM THE NEEDY

When I was dying
You brought me life
You gave me a smile
To keep me alive.
When I was crying
You wiped out my tears
You set me fee
From all my fears.
When I was hopeless
You gave me hope,
With all life's pressures
You made me cope.
When I was lonely,
You sat by my side,
Your words of encouragement
Restored my lost pride.

30. CARE FOR US

When the time comes
We falter like flowers
Dying in the sun
Falling in the storm.
When the time comes
We grow boney thin
Losing our hair;
Looking so frail,
Our bodies cannot cope in the fight against AIDS.
When the time comes
We long for your aid,
We thirst for your love.
When the time comes
Don't despise us,
Don't giggle at our sight
We crave for your help
We cry for your tears;
We may have erred but please we still need your care.

31. WORKERS CRY

You work and sweat
They just sit and talk
Squeezing from you a favor
While you tire and labor.
They get fatter while you get thinner
They want to live on you, but never for you.
Life for them is a celebration,
sweetness never sweated for.
They say sweat is salty
And salt is bitter.
They cry for sugar
Saying it is better,
But nature's law states,
Once and for all,
'There's no sweet without sweat.'

32. ROPE OF HOPE

Do not live on dope,
For you have to climb up life's slope.
Don't drown deep down the alcoholic sea,
Learn to swim and set yourself free,
Time is now to glitter and glee.
Dodge the double troubles
Ensure none of the trouble doubles,
For we live in a world so full of squabbles.
Give up all smokes and dopes,
Freely you shall climb up life's steep slopes.

33. NO LONGER AT EASE

AIDS is a ring of fire
Burning hot
With a killer's desire.
AIDS is a slavery chain
Tight on the neck
Leaving many crying in pain.
AIDS is a killer disease
Silently claiming us soul after soul
Things are no longer at ease.

34. LOST AFRICAN GIRL

My lost African girl,
When I don't kiss your lips
And hold you by your golden hips
You call me ignorant
- Ignorant of modern love.
When I don't touch your breasts
And attend to your expensive tastes
You call me selfish
- Selfish in the game of love.
Because I can't use forks and knives
And take you on romantic jives
You call me anti-social
- Anti social in a world of change.
Because I am not dressed in style
You keep me waiting for a while.
I have to chase you for a mile,
while you shoot me a treacherous smile.

You paint your finger nails,
And do your hair in curls
You paint your lips
And always swing your golden hips.
Your dressing is a scare
And you don't seem to care,
Truly you are a lost African girl.
You've ignored the wisdom of the *chisungu** drums,
You say they are just noise to your eardrums.
You've discarded the *chitenge*** from your waist,
exposing your thighs on no request.
See the way your ageing mother cries,
Can't you pity her swollen tearful eyes?
You are not like her in her prime,
So she cries for you all the time.
My lost African girl
You know my love for you so well,
But cursed be that vulture,
that devours our culture,
- A culture lost through *'Euro-Americanemia'*.

*A usually colorful cloth used by women to cover the lower part of the body.
** Refers to virginity and the ceremony to celebrate it.

❖

35. THIS LIFE

(i)

This life flows like a stream
Swiftly and softly
Clapping against the rocks.
This life blows like a wind
Breezing gently,
kissing the leaves.
This life begins to blow at birth
Flows through growth
And drops at death
Yes, so deep into the earth.

(ii)

It is not all the time
That all words come out in rhyme
There are times we stumble and fall
And cry when we lose it all.
It's all like this in life
Where we face much pain and strife
Nevertheless, enjoy your life!

❖

36. GIRLS OF THE NIGHT

Girls at a the dark corner
Just where is your pride and honor?
Girls in the dark street
Just who are you expecting to meet?
You spend nights by the roadside,
Hoping to get a free ride.
You strip tease to on-coming car lights,
Offering drivers some obscene sights.
You wish them to come to a halt,
And offer you the lifts you've so much sought.
You wish they could take you on hire,
To quench your lustful desire.
Girls of the night
Living in the oldest profession,
Come and make a confession.
Quit the dark corner,
To restore your pride and honor
Quit that life of filth
For the sake of love and health.

37. HUNGRY SOIL

(i)

Grave Waste

Hungry soil
Why do I toil
In order to obtain my oil?
It's a waste of energy.
I am a child of clay
So I never came to stay.
Soon I'll have to depart
And this pains my heart.
It's meaningless this materialistic life,
To be born
To gain education,
Employment,
Wealth,
Fame,
Prestige,
But all to a grave waste
For the hungry soil calls my name
And waits to swallow me.

(ii)

Old Serpent of Sodom

Swallow me not
Old serpent
I am a child of God.
Spit me out of Babylon
the sick Babylon which has enslaved me in evil.
Watch out!
The Sodom of yesterday
Is very much alive today.
There's decay in morals;
Prostitution,
Adultery,
Fornication,
Oh what shame!
"Lord!" I cry,
Redeem me from Sodom
The weakness of my mind tortures me
This Babylon torments me
The chains of drunkenness are much tighter.

Oh lord I'm sick and tired!
Yesterday you rained fire on Sodom
And she perished
But today she has resurrected.
I fear for my tomorrow,
My soul dwells in sorrow.

38. A TRAGIC ENDING

The kisses, so sweet
Set a fire through you,
Burning you alight with lust and passion.
The touch, so tender
Set you aflame
Burning brightly with trust and fashion.
The union and the fusion
Gave you a rare warmth and wetness
Setting both of you high on cloud nine.
The sensation you felt
Gave you false hope,
Fooling you that all was fine,
The tears you shed today
Are the prices you have to pay.
You wasted your lives
Through carefree jives.
Come to think of it,
You risked your precious souls
Ignoring the condom calls
Today your life story has a tragic ending…

www.ingramcontent.com/pod-product-compliance
Ingram Content Group UK Ltd.
Pitfield, Milton Keynes, MK11 3LW, UK
UKHW041905190726
13854UKWH00003B/1093

9 781471 690273